PETE'S
MEAT
MARKET

WHAT HAPPENS TO A HAMBURGER

by Paul Showers

illustrated by Anne Rockwell

THOMAS Y. CROWELL COMPANY   NEW YORK

LET'S-READ-AND-FIND-OUT SCIENCE BOOKS

Editors: *DR. ROMA GANS,* Professor Emeritus of Childhood Education, Teachers College, Columbia University
DR. FRANKLYN M. BRANLEY, Chairman and Astronomer of The American Museum-Hayden Planetarium

Air Is All Around You

Animals in Winter

A Baby Starts to Grow

Bees and Beelines

Before You Were a Baby

The Big Dipper

Big Tracks, Little Tracks

Birds at Night

Birds Eat and Eat and Eat

The Bottom of the Sea

The Clean Brook

Down Come the Leaves

A Drop of Blood

Ducks Don't Get Wet

The Emperor Penguins

Find Out by Touching

Fireflies in the Night

Flash, Crash, Rumble, and Roll

Floating and Sinking

Follow Your Nose

Glaciers

Gravity Is a Mystery

Hear Your Heart

High Sounds, Low Sounds

How a Seed Grows

How Many Teeth?

How You Talk

Hummingbirds in the Garden

Icebergs

In the Night

It's Nesting Time

Ladybug, Ladybug, Fly Away Home

The Listening Walk

*Look at Your Eyes**

A Map Is a Picture

The Moon Seems to Change

My Five Senses

My Hands

My Visit to the Dinosaurs

North, South, East, and West

Rain and Hail

Rockets and Satellites

Salt

Sandpipers

Seeds by Wind and Water

Shrimps

Snow Is Falling

Spider Silk

Starfish

*Straight Hair, Curly Hair**

The Sun: Our Nearest Star

The Sunlit Sea

A Tree Is a Plant

Upstairs and Downstairs

Watch Honeybees with Me

What Happens to a Hamburger

What I Like About Toads

What Makes a Shadow?

What Makes Day and Night

*What the Moon Is Like**

Where Does Your Garden Grow?

Where the Brook Begins

Why Frogs Are Wet

The Wonder of Stones

*Your Skin and Mine**

*AVAILABLE IN SPANISH

L.C. Card 70-106578

ISBN 0-690-87540-1
   0-690-87541-X (LB)

3   4   5   6   7   8   9   10

I like to eat.

1

I like bread

and pears

and celery

and steak.

I like carrots

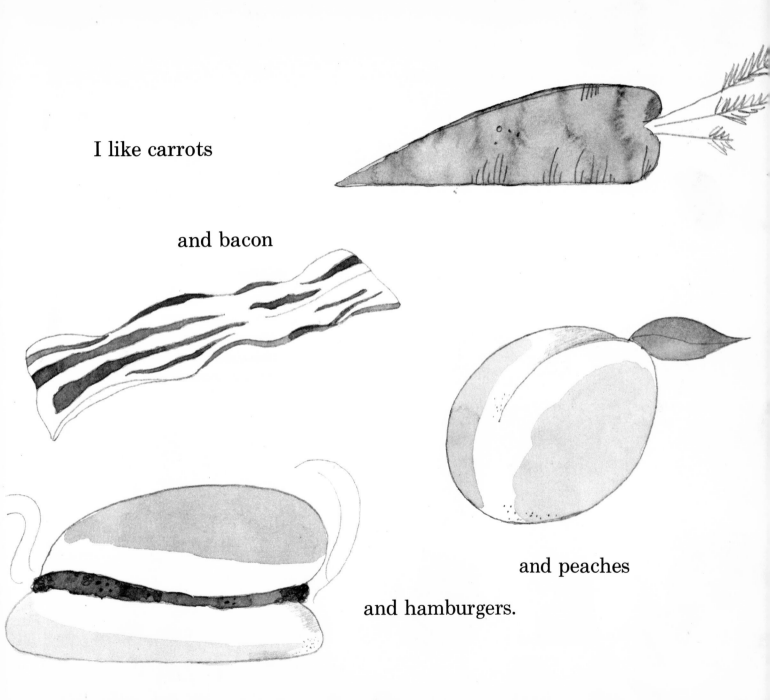

and bacon

and peaches

and hamburgers.

3

I like orange juice and milk and tomato juice and soda.
What do you like?

Good food makes you strong and healthy.
Your body uses food in different ways.

It uses some of the food you eat to keep you warm.

It turns other food into solid muscles.

Some kinds of food are used to make strong bones and hard teeth.

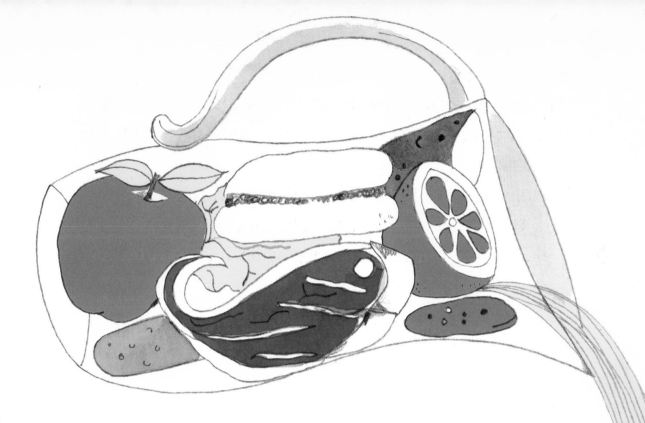

Before your body can do these things, it has to change
   the food.
Solid foods like hamburgers and potatoes have to be
   changed into liquids.
Liquids like milk and orange juice have to be changed,
   too.
When you change the food you eat, you are digesting
   it.

Put two lumps of sugar in an empty glass.
Take a wooden spoon and pound the lumps with the
 handle.
Pound them until they are broken up into powder.
Now pour some water in the glass and stir.
Keep stirring until the sugar powder has disappeared.

Take a sip of water. Can you taste the sugar?
The sugar has disappeared, but it is still there.
It has broken up into millions of tiny pieces.
Your eye cannot see them but your tongue can taste
    them.

When you digest your food, you break it up into millions of very tiny pieces.

You start to do this as soon as you take a bite to eat.

Digestion begins in your mouth when you chew.

You break up the food with your teeth.

Get a piece of raw carrot and a plate.

Take a bite of carrot and chew it twenty times.

Spit out the carrot onto the edge of the plate.

Take another bite. Chew it forty times.

Spit out that mouthful on the other side of the plate.

Can you see the difference?

The longer you chew food, the smaller the pieces will be.

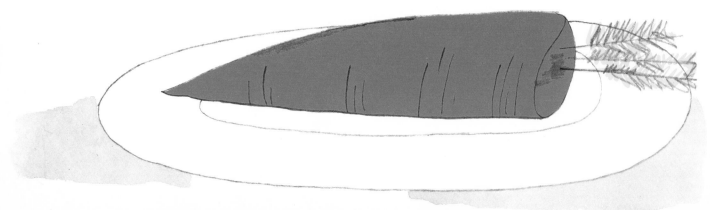

Something else helps to break up food in your mouth.
It is a fluid. Some people call it spit. Its correct name
is saliva.
Whenever you take a bite of food, saliva pours into
your mouth.
You say your mouth is watering.

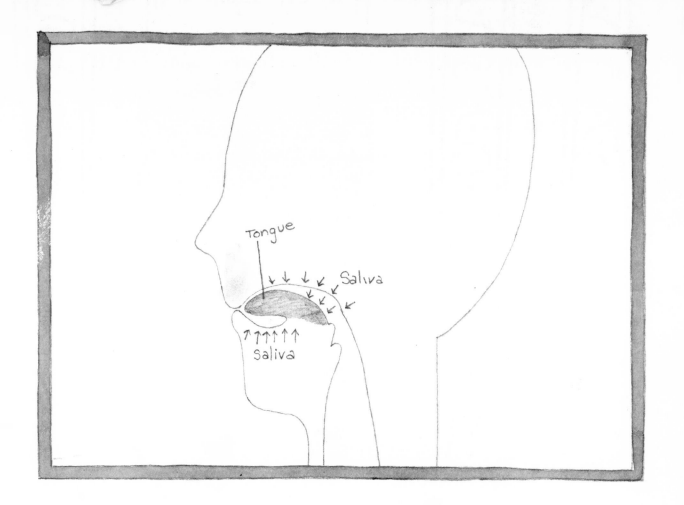

Saliva comes from little openings in your cheeks and
  under your tongue.
Sometimes saliva pours into your mouth even before
  you take a bite.
The smell of food will start it.

Take a good sniff of a box of chocolates.

Sniff a jar of pickles.

What other kind of food makes your mouth water?

16

After you have chewed your food, you swallow it.
Your epiglottis closes. It is a door that keeps food
from going into your lungs.
Your throat squeezes together when you swallow.
It pushes the food down into your esophagus.
Another name for esophagus is gullet.
Your gullet is a tube that leads from the back of your
mouth to your stomach.
There are muscles in your gullet that squeeze
together.

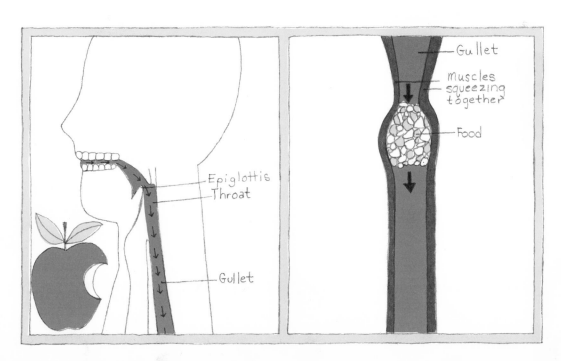

They push food into your stomach.
Sometimes when you don't chew long enough, you can
    feel the food in your gullet.
It feels like a heavy lump going down.
As a matter of fact, it *is* a lump.
The pieces of food are too big.

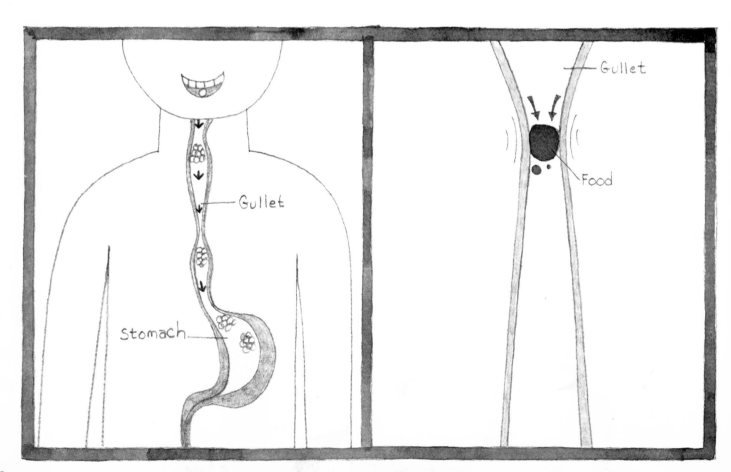

You did not chew long enough.
Next time don't be in such a hurry before you swallow.

Your stomach is a tube like your gullet.
But there is a difference.
Your stomach can stretch like a balloon.
When you eat, your stomach stretches to hold the
food.
It looks something like this when it is full.

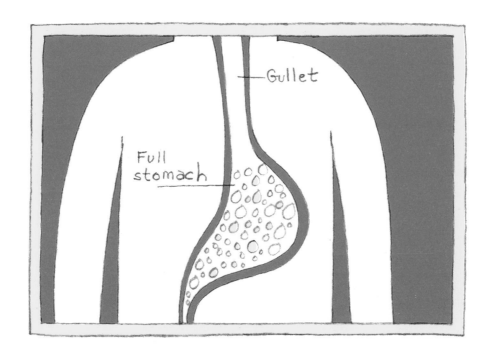

Your stomach has muscles like your gullet.
They can squeeze together.

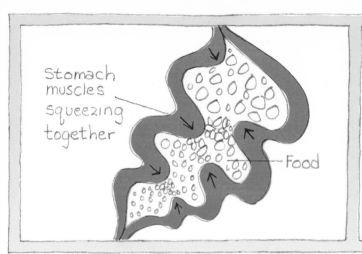
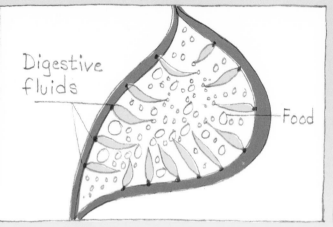

After you swallow your dinner, your stomach closes
   at each end.
The food cannot get out. The muscles begin to
   squeeze.
The food is mashed and stirred together.
Your stomach has fluids in it like the saliva in your
   mouth.
They are called digestive fluids.
They pour in from openings in the sides of the
   stomach.
They help to break up the food into smaller and
   smaller pieces.

Food stays in your stomach for several hours.

Some kinds of food stay only about two hours.

Other kinds stay longer.

The food stays until all the lumps have been broken
up.

It is like a thick soup.

It is made of millions and millions of tiny pieces.

But digestion has just begun.

The tiny pieces must be made smaller.

This happens in the intestines.

There are two intestines—
the small intestine and the large intestine.

They are really one single, long tube.

This tube is coiled up inside you like a pile of heavy
rope.

It is about twenty-one feet long.

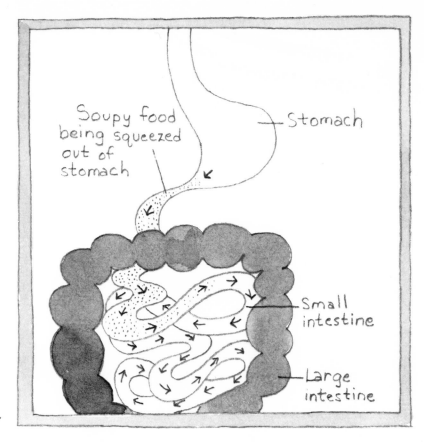

Most of the tube is narrow and is called the small intestine.

The last four or five feet are much bigger around.

This part of the tube is called the large intestine.

The soupy food is squeezed into the small intestine from the stomach.

More digestive fluids are mixed with the food in the
  small intestine.
These fluids break up the food into very tiny pieces
  called molecules.
You cannot see a molecule with an ordinary micro-
  scope.
It is too small.

You cannot weigh a molecule on any scale.
It is too small.
A molecule is so small it can slip through a piece of
  paper without making a hole.

The food molecules pass through the sides of the small intestine.

They move into your blood.

Then your blood carries them to every part of your body.

The part of the food that is not digested in the small intestine is squeezed into the large intestine. From here more molecules pass into the bloodstream.

Your body does not need all of the food you eat.

You get rid of the unused food when you go to the toilet.

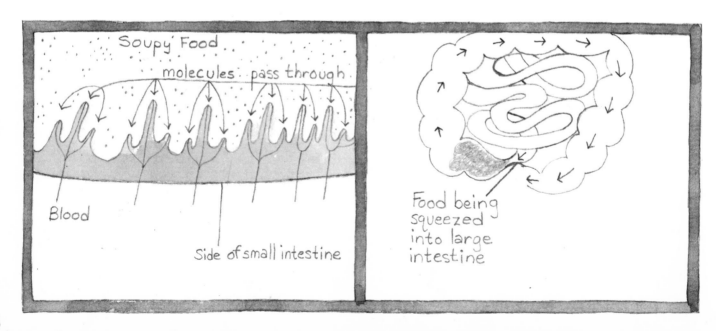

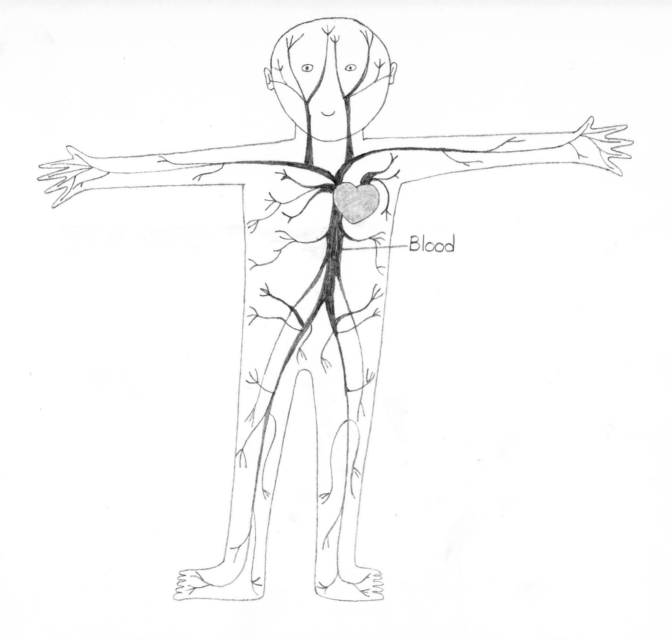

Blood

Blood carries the food molecules you need to all parts of your body.

It carries molecules from hamburger
and butter
and scrambled eggs
and your breakfast cereal

—to your muscles to make them stronger.

29

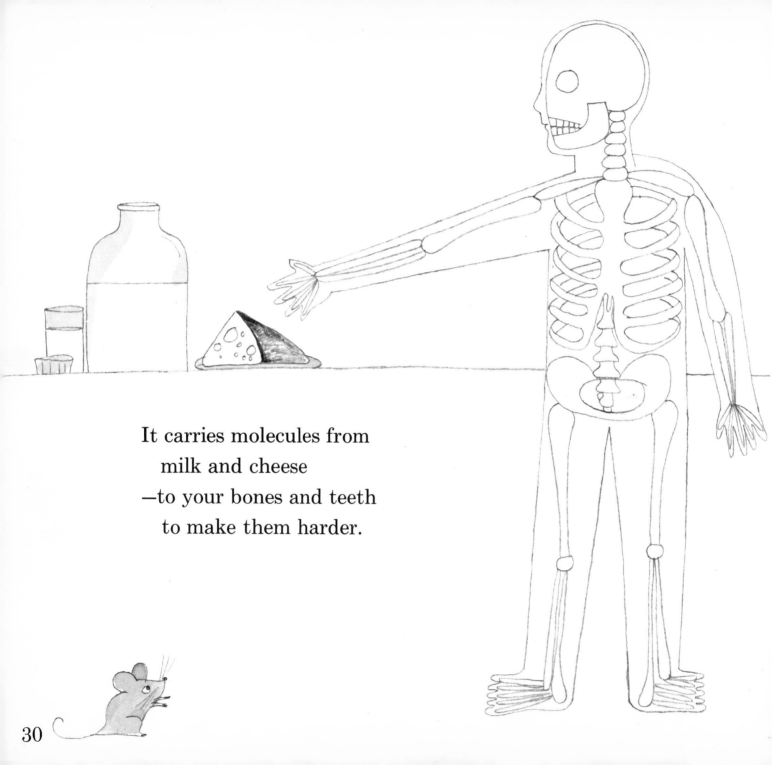

It carries molecules from
milk and cheese
—to your bones and teeth
to make them harder.

It carries molecules from bread
and candy bars and chocolate

—to every part of your body to keep you warm—

and jumping.

ABOUT THE AUTHOR

PAUL SHOWERS is a newspaperman and writer of more than a dozen books for young readers. His first job was with the Detroit *Free Press*; later he worked on the New York *Herald Tribune*. During World War II he served in the Air Corps for a year, then joined the staff of *Yank*, the Army weekly. Since the war, with the exception of a brief stint with the New York *Sunday Mirror*, he has been on the staff of the Sunday *New York Times*.

Mr. Showers was born in Sunnyside, Washington, received his B.A. degree from the University of Michigan, and now lives in New York.

ABOUT THE ILLUSTRATOR

ANNE ROCKWELL brings her "habit of careful research" to each of the varied projects she undertakes.

Mrs. Rockwell has illustrated over a dozen books, many of which she also wrote. Her books have won many honors and awards. Mrs. Rockwell has been drawing and painting all her life. Although she is primarily a self-taught artist, she studied sculpture for three years at the Sculpture Center, and etching and engraving at the Pratt Graphic Arts Center in New York.

Anne Rockwell and her husband now live in Connecticut with their three children to whom she is always explaining "how everything works . . . including of course, what happens to food when we eat it."